*hello*

# Quebec

## GLC❖SILVER BURDETT
### PUBLISHERS

## ELMA SCHEMENAUER

Canada Rainbow Series
Cities

© 1986 **GLC Publishers Limited**
  115 Nugget Avenue
  Agincourt, Ontario  M1S 3B1

**Canadian Cataloguing in Publication Data**
Schemenauer, Elma.
  Hello Quebec city

(Canada rainbow series)
For use in schools.
Includes index.
ISBN 0-88874-258-4 (bound). - ISBN 0-88874-242-8 (pbk.). -
ISBN 0-88874-269-X (set, bound). - ISBN 0-88874-267-3
(set, pbk.)

1. Québec (Quebec) - Juvenile literature.
I. Title. II. Series.

FC2946.33.S33 1986      j971.4'471      C85-099811-5
F1054.5.Q3S33 1986

## The Author
Elma Schemenauer is originally from Saskatchewan, and is presently living in Ontario. She has taught school in Saskatchewan and Nova Scotia, and has written a number of educational books for children.

Project Editor & Photo Research: *Deborah Lonergan*
Permissions Editor: *Estelle McGurk*
Design & Art Direction: *Holly Fisher & Associates*
Manuscript Reviewer: *Marianna O'Gallagher*
Printed & Bound in Canada by: *Friesen Printers Ltd., Altona, Manitoba*

**CREDITS**
*Cover Photo:* P.J. Frith/Hot Shots; Archives Nationales du Québec, Fonds Livernois, Quebec, Couvent des Urselines, N78-5-10-18, pg. 15, Fonds Wurtele, Quebec, Basse-ville, A-31, pg. 17, Collection Initiale, Jacques Cartier 1491-1557, GH473-63, pg. 13; Department of Regional Industrial Expansion photo, pgs. 6, 9, 10, 21, 23, 24, 25, 28; Deborah Drew-Brook-Cormack and Allan Cormack, pg. 14; J. G. Graphics, pg. 7; La Ville de Québec, pgs, 8, 11, 12, 22; L.P. Vallee/Public Archives Canada/C-35634, pg. 20; Picture Division, Public Archives Canada/C-4501, pg. 16; Tourisme - Québec, pgs. 18, 19, 26, 29.

*hello*
# Quebec

# Contents

Bonhomme says *"Bienvenue à Québec."* That's French for "Welcome to Quebec." Every winter, Bonhomme welcomes visitors to Quebec City's exciting *Carnaval*. The jolly giant snowman romps through the city streets. When people see him coming, they wave and toot red plastic trumpets.

Bonhomme's city is very old. It is Canada's leading showcase of history. Quebec City is also the capital of the province of Quebec. (Quebec City is often called just Quebec.)

*Meet Bonhomme. Why is he the star of Quebec City's winter carnival?*

**CANADA**

SCALE
km  0  500  1000

QUEBEC

Quebec City

Like Bonhomme, Quebec City's people are known for their
*joie de vivre*, or enjoyment of life. Altogether, there are about
570 000 of them. About 95% speak French as their first
language. Of the remaining 5%, many are of Irish
background.

Quebec's people are proud of their beautiful old city. It is
on the north bank of the St. Lawrence River, about 1400 km
inland from the ocean. Southwest of Quebec, towards
Montreal, are flat rich farmlands. Northeast of Quebec are
round–topped mountains. In the autumn, the countryside
blazes with red and orange sugar maples.

*Quebec City from the St. Lawrence River. Can you see the dark-green cliff separating Lower Town from Upper Town?*

Clip, clop, clip, clop. Horse-drawn wagons called *calèches* wind their way through narrow cobblestone streets. Bong, bong, bong. Church bells ring from stone **steeples** over 300 years old. Hop, skip, jump. A small girl skips home across a sunny city square. Under her arm is a long loaf of French bread for her family's dinner.

This is old Quebec. It is a "split level" city. Lower Town squeezes in between the river and a steep cliff. Upper Town sits 61 m higher, at the top of the cliff.

8

To get from Lower Town to Upper Town, you can walk up the Champlain Stairs. (They are often called the Breakneck Stairs!) Or you can get up the easy way. You can ride in a modern outdoor elevator. In French it is called the *Acenseur*. The entrance to the *Acenseur* is in the home of an early French explorer, Louis Jolliet.

The *Acenseur* lets you out on a boardwalk called the Dufferin Terrace. It runs along just below the top of the cliff. Near by is the beautiful Chateau Frontenac. It is Quebec City's most famous hotel.

*The Chateau Frontenac. Can you see the Ascenseur going up the cliff at the right of the picture?*

The boardwalk leads you along the riverside walls of the Citadel. The Citadel is a large star–shaped fort. It is built on Quebec City's highest point. Boom! If you're there at noon, you can hear the Citadel's big gun firing. Past the Citadel along the boardwalk, you reach Battlefields Park. Here in 1759, French and English soldiers fought a great battle that changed Canada's history forever.

Today, however, grassy Battlefields Park is a place to play catch, ride bikes, and fly kites. In the park, you can also visit the Quebec Museum. It has many interesting displays of French Canadian arts and crafts, paintings, and beautiful silver work.

*The Citadel, built on Quebec City's highest point.*

*Restaurant aux Anciens Canadiens. Part of it used to be a house, one of the oldest in the province.*

Are you hungry from all that walking? In the streets of Upper Town, you can eat at one of Quebec City's many fine restaurants. Try a special Quebec dish — pea soup with hot crusty bread, pork pie, or maybe duck in maple syrup.

While you're in Upper Town, you can stroll through the *Rue du Trésor*. It is an outdoor art **gallery** where young Quebec artists sell their paintings. You can visit the Wax Museum with its many colourful scenes from Canada's history. And you can puzzle over the Golden Dog carved above the post office building door. What does the Golden Dog carving mean? Nobody knows for sure. It's a mystery!

*A gate in Quebec City's old stone wall. Why are there now many buildings outside the wall?*

Walking in Upper Town, you notice a thick stone wall around the old part of the city. Like many European cities, Quebec was built inside a protecting wall. However, the growing city spilled over its wall years ago.

Quebec City now has many more streets and buildings *outside* its walls than inside. Among them are modern hotels, office buildings, shopping malls, and homes. Even though Quebec City has long since outgrown its wall, Quebeckers are still proud of the wall. They love to point out that Quebec is North America's only walled city north of Mexico.

Long ago, there was no stone wall at what is now Quebec
City. There was no Upper Town or Lower Town. The great
cliff overlooking the St. Lawrence River was the site of a
Native village, Stadacona. The Native Iroquoian Indians lived
in wooden **longhouses**. They grew corn, beans, and squash.
In their swift canoes, they traded up and down the river.

Then in 1535, along came French explorer Jacques Cartier.
He visited and traded with the Native people. But he did not
start a lasting French settlement.

JACQUES CARTIER 1491–1557

*French explorer
Jacques Cartier.
Can you find the
Iroquoian village
of Stadacona
(Stadaconé)
on the map?*

*Champlain's first fort at Quebec. He called it the Abitation.*

It was French explorer Samuel de Champlain who began the first lasting French settlement on the St. Lawrence. In 1608 — in what is now Lower Town — Champlain built his first fort. It included two dwellings and a storehouse. All around was a fence of strong sharp posts, called a *palisade*.

Champlain named his fort *kebec*. This was the Native word for "place where the river narrows." The fort became the centre of a fur-trading settlement. As more French people arrived, the settlement climbed the cliff and spread out on top. (This is the area we know today as Upper Town.)

Louis Hébert was the first French farmer at the *kebec* (though Native people had farmed there for years). Louis cleared land. He grew corn, beans, peas, and wheat to feed the people of Champlain's settlement. Louis' wife, Marie, was very interested in the area's Native children. She spent a lot of time teaching them. She hoped they would become Christians.

Almost from the beginning, *kebec* (or Quebec) was a centre for the Roman Catholic faith in North America. The settlement's people soon built schools, **convents**, **monasteries**, and many churches.

*Quebec City's Ursuline Convent. Almost from the beginning, the city was a centre for the Roman Catholic faith.*

15

During those years the French were not the only European settlers in North America. The English were there too — a constant **challenge** to New France. At last, in 1759, came the famous battle on the Plains of Abraham (now Battlefields Park).

General James Wolfe led his red-coated English soldiers. General Louis-Joseph Montcalm led the French. The battle was brief but bitter. The English won. Soon Quebec — as well as the rest of New France — was under British rule.

*Death of Wolfe, Battle of Plains of Abraham, 1759. George B. Campion did this painting.*

*Quebec City in the 1880s. Why do you think the city became important as a port?*

French Canadians did not lose everything on the Plains of Abraham. It was not the end of their way of life. Under the new British government, they still kept their language and religion. They kept their land and many of their laws.

In the years following 1759, Quebec City grew. It was a centre for selling timber. The city also became important as a port for **vessels** from around the world. In 1867, along with its province, it became part of a new nation, Canada. Quebec City was chosen as the province's capital.

17

*"Je me souviens."* This is an important motto for Quebeckers. It means "I remember." The people of Quebec City never forget the glories of New France. All over the city are reminders of the key role that Quebec played in Canada's history.

*Place Royale* in Lower Town is where Champlain built his first fort. On the exact spot stands a church called *Notre Dame des Victoires* (Our Lady of Victories). The church's main altar is carved in the shape of a fort.

*Notre Dame des Victoires. Why is this church especially important to Quebeckers?*

*Louis Hébert stands at the top of this monument. Below him is Guillaume Couillard, Hébert's son-in-law and first farmhand.*

In the heart of Upper Town, you meet Champlain himself — or at least his statue! Hat in hand, the hardy explorer salutes Quebec. A stone angel below him announces the "arrival of a hero."

In a park in the east of the city is a **monument** to the memory of Louis and Marie Hébert. Quebec's first French farmer, Louis offers God the first sheaf of wheat grown in Canada. Marie is shown teaching children the story of the Christian faith.

*Hôtel-Dieu Hospital in the 1870s. How does it look different from the way hospitals look today?*

Brave General Montcalm is not forgotten either. In fact, his dried-up yellowish skull has a place of honour at the Ursuline Convent. This convent was started in 1639. It is known as North America's oldest school for women.

Just a few blocks north is the *Hôtel-Dieu* Hospital. It is known as North America's oldest hospital. There visitors can see displays of old medical equipment. Included is an operating gown dyed red to hide blood stains! There are also wooden shoes. These were to protect the feet in case the **surgeon** dropped one of his knives.

"Rest in the Forest" is the name of a beautiful sculpture. It is at Quebec's Parliament Building. The artist created the work to honour the Native people, first to live in the area.

The Parliament Building is where members of Quebec's provincial government meet. They deal with matters affecting the whole province. They are the only French-speaking provincial government in Canada.

*Quebec's provincial government leaders meet in the Parliament Building in Quebec City.*

Quebec city government meets at *l'Hôtel de Ville*, or City Hall. Since 1970 this government has been called the Quebec Urban Community. It is made up of a mayor and 21 councillors. The councillors are from 21 districts. These districts include the main city of Quebec, and other smaller communities around it.

The mayor and councillors deal with matters affecting the whole area. For instance, they discuss how much tax to charge home owners and businesses. They also talk about how to use this tax money to pay for city services such as parks, street lights, and **transportation**.

*Quebec City government leaders meet at City Hall. What are some of the things they discuss?*

*Two-wheeled calèches and four-wheeled victorias wait to take tourists around old Quebec.*
*How do most Quebeckers travel around their city?*

Most Quebeckers find their city easy and quick to drive around in. Buses also help people travel around the city. In the old part of the city, there are horse–drawn wagons called *calèches*. These are used by tourists.

"Look for the red and white snowflake at the bus stop." In winter many Quebeckers like to go skiing. The city runs a special Skibus service into the nearby mountains. The snowflake design tells people where to catch a Skibus for a day of fun in the snow.

*An ice climber at Quebec City's winter Carnaval. What safety equipment is the climber wearing? What is winter like in Quebec?*

When Jacques Cartier visited the Quebec area back in the 1500s, he was shocked at how cold the winters were. They were far colder than in France. Cartier joked that his sailors' words froze on their lips. The words hung silent in the air. It was only in spring that they thawed out so people could hear them!

In fact, Quebec City's climate is no harsher than that of many other parts of Canada. Average January temperature is about –11°C. Usually there is a lot of snow in winter. Average July temperature is about 19°C. Usually summers are sunny and quite dry.

Quebec's people are known for their playful sense of winter. They make it fun. They ski, skate, toboggan, snowshoe, and ice fish. They love to play hockey, and also to cheer on their famous hockey team, the Quebec Nordiques.

In February the jolly giant snowman, Bonhomme, hosts the biggest winter fun of all. It's *Carnaval*. Visitors come from all over Canada and the U.S. There are parades, dances, snow sculptures, a snow castle, and winter sports of all kinds. There are even daring canoe races among the floating ice floes of the St. Lawrence River!

*At Carnaval, daring canoeists race over and around floating chunks of ice in the St. Lawrence River.*

*The Grand Théâtre de Quebec with its white pillars and slanted roof. What could you do there?*

Quebec City's people celebrate summer too. Folk singers, jugglers, and puppeteers perform in the streets, especially in the old part of the city. Every year there is a music and arts event known as *Festival d'Été* (Festival of Summer).

Quebeckers are especially proud of their new *Grand Théâtre de Québec*. It features concerts, plays, and **opera**. It is also the home of the Quebec **Symphony Orchestra**, Canada's oldest. Quebec City's *Université Laval* and *Université du Québec* are also important to the city's **cultural** life.

As you might think, many people in Quebec City have jobs taking care of tourists. For instance, some offer "bed and breakfast" in their homes, especially inside the city walls. Others are tour guides, restaurant workers, and hotel employees. Most of these people's jobs are classed as *services*.

A lot of Quebec City people also work in shops and stores. Their jobs are classed in the *trade* group. Since Quebec City is the province's capital, government is a third major source of jobs. Thousands of the city's people work for the provincial government as **civil servants**.

*Pie graph showing jobs in Quebec City. Which "piece of the job pie" is the biggest? Which is second biggest?*

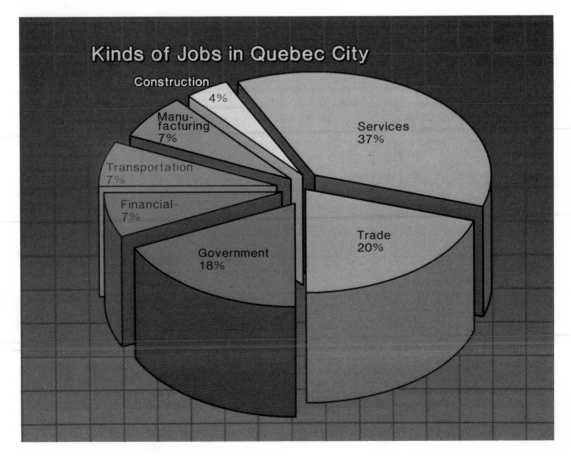

Kinds of Jobs in Quebec City

Construction 4%
Manufacturing 7%
Transportation 7%
Financial- 7%
Government 18%
Services 37%
Trade 20%

**Manufacturing** keeps about 7% of Quebec City's working people busy. Some of them work in sawmills. Some make such things as doors, windows, metal products, and food and beverage products. Some make pulp and paper products such as cardboard and newsprint. An interesting fact is that Quebec City people make the paper on which *The New York Times* newspaper is printed.

Among Quebec City people who work in transportation, a number have jobs at the harbour. They take care of ships and goods travelling along the St. Lawrence River and out to sea. The port of Quebec is open all year round. Vessels can always get through if they have strong enough hulls. However, they often need the help of icebreakers.

*Loading goods onto a ship at Quebec City's harbour. What other jobs might people do at the harbour?*

*Old and new buildings in Quebec City. How do the people feel about their city's rapid growth in recent years?*

Super highways, housing developments, shopping centres . . . since the 1960s, the new part of Quebec City has been growing fast. There have also been changes inside the old walls.

Some Quebeckers worry about growing too fast. How can they create a sleek modern city without destroying the old one? *"Je me souviens."* This motto will continue to be important to Quebec. The city is still Canada's "showcase of history." But it is also finding exciting new ways to face the challenges of the future.

# Glossary

**challenge** — A call to take part in a contest or struggle (p. 16).

**civil servant** — A person who has been hired by the government. Civil servants do many different kinds of jobs for the government. For example, they are clerks, secretaries, office managers, computer programmers, scientists (p. 27).

**convent** — A building in which a community of nuns live and work according to certain religious rules (p. 15).

**cultural** — Having to do with culture. Culture is the way of living and/or the artistic products of a group of people (p. 26).

**gallery** — A room or building where works of art are shown (p. 11).

**longhouse** — A type of large wooden dwelling built by some Native people of North America, especially Iroquoians (p. 13).

**manufacturing** — The producing or making of things, especially by machine (p. 28).

**monastery** — A building in which a community of monks or nuns live and work according to certain religious rules (p. 15).

**monument** — Something set up in memory of a person or event; for example, a statue, large stone, or building (p. 19).

**opera** — A kind of play set to music, usually performed by singers (p. 26).

**steeple** — A tower on the top of a church (p. 8).

**surgeon** — A medical doctor who is especially trained to perform operations (p. 20).

**symphony orchestra** — A large group of musicians who play long, usually quite serious pieces of music called symphonies (p. 26).

**transportation** — The method or methods of carrying people and things from one place to another (p. 22).

**vessel** — A ship (p. 17).

# Index